Better Homes and Gardens®

MAKE BELIEVE

Hi! My name is Max.
I have some great projects
to show you—and they're
all about make-believe! We're
going to have lots of fun
making them together.

Inside You'll Find...

Identify the parts of the castle and find the hidden letters.

At the Castle

Hey, look! Max is going to the castle. Can you name the parts of a castle? Look at the picture to find the name of each part.

Flag

Turret

Moat

Drawbridge

Find the Hidden Letters

Look at the words below. Then find the first letter of each word hidden twice in the picture of the castle.

Castle

Flag

Turret

Moat

Drawbridge

Match the small letters in the first column with the capital letters in the second column.

t	Castle
d	Flag
c	Turret
f	Moat
m	Drawbridge

This shoe-box castle will be a "shoo-in" with any king or queen.

A Grand Castle

Max likes to play with his castle. He uses other toys and makes up stories about the people who live there. You can do this, too.

What you'll need...

- 1 shoe box
- Scissors
- 2 pieces of yarn (8 inches long)
- Tape
- White crafts glue
- Four 4½-inch cardboard tubes (toilet paper tubes)
- Construction paper
- Four 4-inch circles of construction paper
- 4 Flags (optional) (see page 30)

1 For the drawbridge, in the middle of 1 long side of the box draw 2 lines from the top of the box to the bottom about 2 inches apart. Cut on the lines. Tape 1 end of 1 piece of yarn to the top of the box. Tape the other end to the end of the drawbridge (see photo). Cut off any extra yarn. Repeat with the other piece of yarn.

2 Glue one cardboard tube to each corner of the shoe box (see photo). Let dry. If desired, glue torn pieces of construction paper to the shoe box for stones (see photo on page 7).

3 Cut a pie-shaped wedge out of each construction paper circle (about ¼ of the circle). Bring the cut ends together and overlap slightly to make a cone shape (see photo). Leave a small opening at the top of the cone. Tape edges to hold. Tape cones on top of each paper tube. If desired, push 1 Flag through the hole in the top of each cone.

Adorn these paper crowns with simple household findings.

Royal Crown

All kings and queens wear pretty crowns, and so can you. What would you do if you were a king or queen? Would you live in a castle? What kind of clothes would you wear?

What you'll need...

- One 9x12-inch piece of construction paper
- Marker or pencil
- Scissors
- Tape
- Crown Jewels (see tip on page 9)

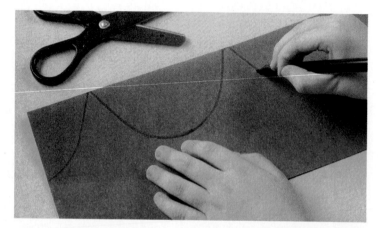

1 Fold the construction paper in half lengthwise. With adult help, use a marker to draw the shape of a crown with 3 points (see photo). Be sure to put the points of the crown on the fold of the paper.

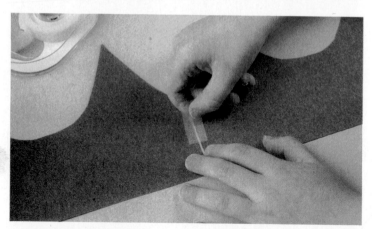

2 Cut out the crown. Separate the crown into 2 pieces. Lay the 2 pieces end-to-end. Tape these 2 ends of the crown together (see photo).

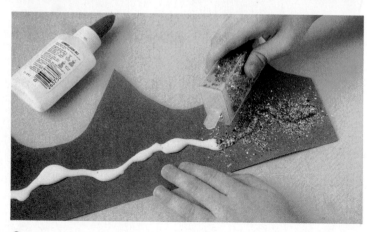

3 Decorate the crown with any of the ideas for Crown Jewels (see photo). If necessary, let dry. Put the crown around your head so it fits comfortably. Tape the other ends of the crown together.

Crown Jewels

Add some razzle-dazzle to your crown by gluing on pretend jewels. Here are some ideas to get you started: glitter, small beads, large pasta shapes, small balls of foil, rickrack, pom-poms, or paper. If none of these are handy, draw jewels on your crown with crayons or markers.

Find the musical instruments and learn about sound.

Wizard Wonders

Elliot is in a jam. He lost all his musical instruments in Max's laboratory. Can you find the bell, cymbals, drum, mandolin, tambourine, trumpet, and xylophone hidden in the picture?

Did you know...

● You can't see sound, but you can hear it. A sound is made when something vibrates, or moves, over and over and over again. Sometimes you can see the object vibrate and sometimes you can't.

● When something vibrates quickly, it makes a high sound. When something vibrates slowly, it makes a low sound. The highness or lowness of sound is called pitch.

● Sound moves in all directions. It moves through air and water. Sound also moves through solids, such as metal and plastic. It moves best through metal.

● What kinds of sounds do the instruments hidden in the picture of Max's laboratory make?

A plain brown paper bag comes to life as a towering hat.

Wizard Hat

Wise wizards always wear their Wizard Hats. That's fun to say. Can you say it fast? If you were a wizard, what kind of magic would you do?

What you'll need...

- Scissors
- 1 large brown paper sack or 1 sheet of heavy gift wrap

- Pencil
- Paints, markers, or stickers

- Tape
- Yarn or string

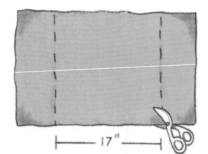

1 Cut out a 17-inch square from the paper sack.

2 With a pencil, round off one corner (as shown). Cut along the line. Paint the hat. Let dry.

3 Bring the sides of the hat together to make a cone shape (as shown). Tape the edges to hold.

4 Trim off the bottom edge of the hat to make it even all the way around.

5 For ties, cut 2 pieces of yarn about 12 inches long. Tape one end of each piece to the inside of the hat (as shown).

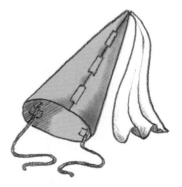

6 If desired, tape a square piece of lightweight fabric, a scarf, or crepe-paper streamers to the point of the hat.

Use pencils and foil to make a spectacular wand.

Magical Wand

Abracadabra and alacawax. Look! The frog turned into Max! If you could change yourself into something else, what would it be? What would it do?

What you'll need...

- 2 unsharpened pencils or 1 wooden dowel about 14 inches long
- Markers or stickers
- Tape
- Foil
- Scissors
- Crinkle ribbon (optional)
- 1 long twist-tie or pipe cleaner

1 You can purchase decorative pencils. Or, decorate pencils with markers, if desired. Tape the ends of the pencils together (see photo). Tear off a 12-inch piece of the foil. Cut the foil into thin strips about ¼ inch wide.

2 Gather the foil strips into a pile. If desired, add curled crinkle ribbon to the pile of foil strips. Fasten the twist-tie around the middle of the strips (see photo). Leave 2 ends of the twist-tie long enough to fasten to one end of the pencils.

This ice-cream drink will tempt little *and* big wizards.

Magic Potion

Bubble and brew, simmer and stew. This nose-tickling beverage is just for you! And, it comes in different colors, too!

What you'll need...

- Pitcher
- ½ cup sugar
- 1 envelope *unsweetened* flavored soft-drink mix
- ½ cup cold water
- Vanilla ice cream
- 6 tall glasses
- One 33.8-ounce bottle (1 liter) lemon-lime carbonated beverage or carbonated water, chilled

1 In the pitcher, dissolve sugar and soft-drink mix in water.

2 Put 1 or 2 scoops of ice cream into each glass.

3 To serve, stir the lemon-lime carbonated beverage into the soft-drink mixture. Pour over the ice cream in glasses. Makes 6 servings.

Count the rocks and look for the hidden elves.

An Enchanted Forest

Once upon a time, Max was walking in an enchanted forest. He was on his way to visit his mischievous elf friends at their cottage. On the way, he was gathering rocks. Can you count the 10 rocks he hasn't found yet? Can you help him find the 5 elves that are hiding?

The salt in the paint makes the rocks glisten.

Glow Stones

Do you know what a Glow Stone is? It's a pretend magic rock. Make believe your stones turn into something else when you say the magic word. What is your secret magic word?

What you'll need...

- Waxed paper, newspaper, or brown kraft paper
- Small rocks
- 1 egg carton
- Paintbrush
- Salt Paint (see page 31)

1 Cover your work surface with waxed paper. Wash and dry the rocks. Turn the egg carton upside down. Place the rocks on the egg carton (see photo). This makes a drying rack for your rocks for Step 2.

2 Paint the rocks with the Salt Paint any way you like (see photo). Let dry.

Treasure Hunting

Have you ever been on a treasure hunt? It's a pretend adventure you go on to look for precious things. You don't have to go far. Your room or backyard is full of treasures. You might find a funny-shaped stick that looks like a magic wand or a pretty leaf you imagine to be a secret treasure map. What treasures would you hunt for? What would you take with you?

An easy-to-build take-off of a gingerbread house.

Cozy Cottage

Yum! These cottages are a sweet treat to eat, and they're fun to build. Would you like to live in a Cozy Cottage? What kinds of candy would you put on your cottage?

What you'll need...

- Waxed paper
- Spatula or table knife
- Canned frosting, chilled
- 5 rectangular graham crackers
- Assorted candies and cookies

1 If desired, cover your work surface with waxed paper. Use 2 graham crackers for the base. Spread lots of frosting on 1 long edge of 1 cracker. Press the other cracker against the frosting (see photo). Spread a thick layer of frosting all over the base.

2 Break the other 3 crackers in half. Spread lots of frosting along 2 opposite edges of each of the cracker squares. To make the walls, stand 2 of the crackers up on the base, unfrosted side down (see photo). Press them together in the corners. Repeat with 2 more crackers, joining all 4 corners to make 4 walls.

3 For the roof, set 1 frosted edge of each remaining cracker on top of opposite walls. Tilt the crackers toward the center of the house till they meet (see photo). (If desired, completely frost the crackers before adding them to the walls.) To decorate the house, spread some frosting on the candies and gently press onto the house.

Ice-Cream-Cone Trees

What could be better than a bright green tree to go with your Cozy Cottage? All you need to do is stir some green food coloring into white frosting. Then spread a thick layer of frosting all over a sugar cone. Decorate the frosted cone with small candies or sprinkle it with powdered sugar.

23

Fanciful Fortune-Tellers

Max's friend, Vera, is dressed up as a fortune-teller. She's going to tell Max's fortune. Look at the pictures. They are not exactly the same. Can you find the 10 things that are different?

A project for stretching kids' imaginations.

Shiny Crystal Ball

Invite your friends over so you can tell their fortunes. First, you'll need to make a Shiny Crystal Ball. Then dress up, if you like. What would you wear if you were a fortune-teller?

What you'll need...

- Plastic margarine tub or frozen whipped topping container
- Stickers or permanent markers (optional)
- Newspaper or brown kraft paper
- Tape
- Foil
- White crafts glue

1 For the base, decorate the plastic margarine tub with stickers, if desired. Roll newspaper into a ball about the size of a softball. Tape the loose ends (see photo).

2 Tear off enough foil to cover the ball of paper. Wrap the foil around the ball of newspaper (see photo). Glue or tape onto the base.

Fortune-Telling

Do you know what it means to tell someone's fortune? It means telling people now what will happen to them later today or tomorrow or next week. You can have fun pretending to tell your friends' fortunes with your Shiny Crystal Ball.

Wave your hands over the ball and pretend you see a picture inside the ball. This pretend picture is the fortune. Maybe you see what your friends will eat for lunch tomorrow. Or that they will find a special treasure on the way home. You might see that you will be friends forever. Whatever pretend fortunes you tell, remember to have fun.

A ritzy ring to wear and a snazzy necklace to eat.

Magic Ring and Necklace

Magic jewelry gives special powers to anyone who wears it. What kind of powers does your jewelry have?

What you'll need...

- One 6-inch piece of pipe cleaner
- Paper plate or construction paper
- White crafts glue
- Beads, foil, glitter, or stickers

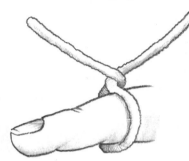

Fold the pipe cleaner in half. Lay your finger in the middle of the pipe cleaner. Wrap the pipe cleaner around your finger. Twist the pipe cleaner together at the top of your finger. Join the ends of the pipe cleaner so they make a circle. If desired, bend the circle toward your finger.

Ring Designs

You can create many different designs for your magic ring. Here are a few ideas for decorations:

- Thread colorful beads onto the pipe cleaner *before* joining ends to make a circle.
- Make a small ball of foil just big enough to

fit inside the circle.
- Cut a circle out of a paper plate or heavy paper the same size as the pipe cleaner circle. Decorate the paper circle with glitter or stickers. Glue the paper circle on top of the pipe cleaner circle. Let dry.

What you'll need...

- One 30-inch piece of shoestring licorice
- Assorted candies and cereal with holes in the center

To make the necklace, tie a loose knot in one end of the licorice. Thread assorted candies and cereal onto licorice. Carefully tie ends of licorice together.

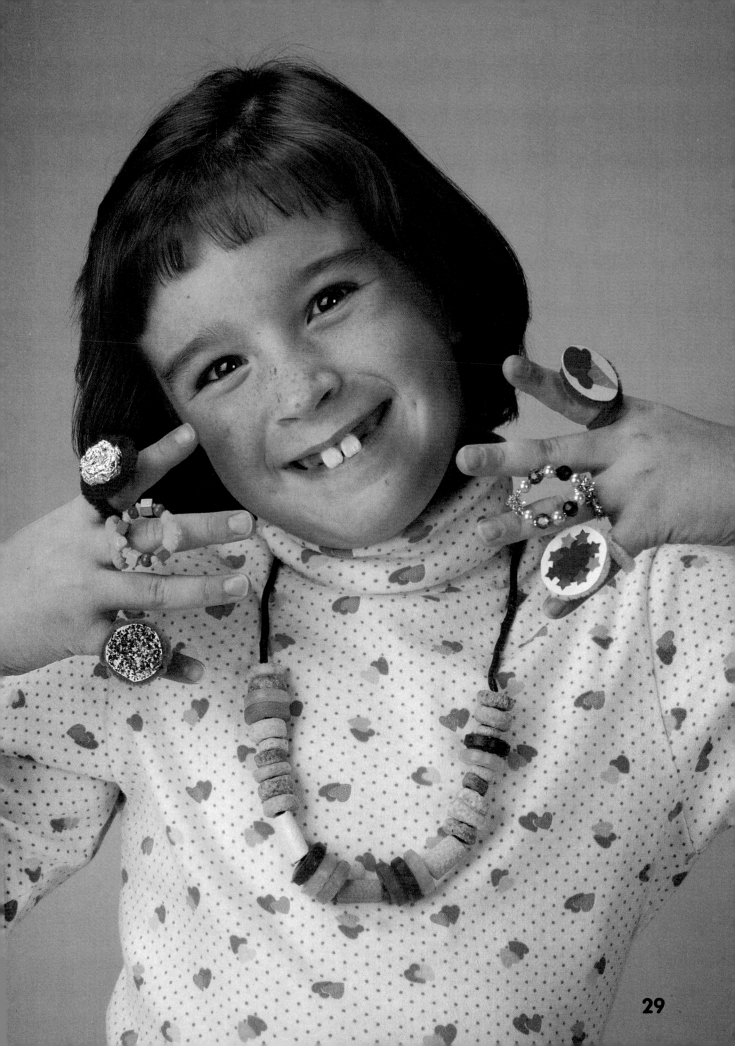

Parents' Pages

We've filled this special section with more activities, recipes, reading recommendations, hints we learned from our kid-testers, and many other helpful tips.

At the Castle

See pages 4 and 5

Besides fiction books, there are many interesting books written about castles and what life was like for the people who lived in them. Spend some time at the library with your children learning about this fascinating part of history.
● Reading suggestion:
Saint George and the Dragon by Margaret Hodges

A Grand Castle

See pages 6 and 7

If you can't find four toilet paper tubes, use paper towel tubes cut in half or gift wrap tubes cut into 4-inch lengths.

For the Flags: Cut four small triangles from construction paper. Then glue or tape the triangles onto the ends of four toothpicks.

Royal Crown

See pages 8 and 9

If you're looking for a way to cheer up little faces, make them kings or queens for a day. Give them a crown and grant them a wish, such as choosing the food for dinner or a movie you can see together.

Wizard Wonders

See pages 10 and 11

Try this simple sound experiment. Fill 3 identical pop bottles with water. Fill one ⅓ full, one ½ full, and one ⅔ full. Blow across the top of each bottle. This vibrates the column of air in the bottle. Which one has the lowest sound? (The bottle with the least water will have the lowest frequency, or pitch.)

Wizard Hat

See pages 12 and 13

Complete the wizard costume with a cotton-ball beard.

To make the beard, cut a triangle from a 9-inch paper plate. Punch a hole in two corners of the triangle. Attach one end of a pipe cleaner to each hole. Adjust the other end to fit over the child's ears. Use white crafts glue to glue cotton balls to the front of the triangle.

Dress-Up Duds

Most children like to imagine they're a favorite real or pretend character they've seen or read about, or that they're a "grown-up." A favorite prop for this kind of play is dress-up clothes.

To entice your children, start a collection of adult clothes they can play with. Capes and hats are among the favored choices of children. A purse, shoes, ties, fancy dresses, and shirts are other suggestions. (If you're in search of great dress-up treasures and have exhausted your home supply, check out the garage sales or second-hand stores in your area.)

Look for a special place to keep these clothes so the children know these clothes are meant to be tried on and played with. Let them decorate the box or carton you're going to use with markers, crayons, construction paper, or gift wrap.

As you assemble this wardrobe, keep in mind that many children don't like to wear clothes that have to be pulled over their heads. Something that slips over the front of their clothes is less restrictive and easier to put on and take off.

Magical Wand

See pages 14 and 15

This project was one of the most successful with our kid-testers—and their parents! Everyone likes listening to the magical rustling sound of the wand when it's shaken. During testing, we found that lightweight generic foil is easier to work with. And it makes a better rustling sound than the heavier name brands.

Magic Potion

See pages 16 and 17

This potion fills your head with visions of dancing fruit.

Fizzberries

> 1 10-ounce package frozen sliced strawberries
> 1 8-ounce carton strawberry yogurt
> ½ cup orange juice
> 1 12-ounce can lemon-lime carbonated beverage

Thaw the berries. In a blender container, combine berries, yogurt, and orange juice. Cover and blend till smooth. Stir in lemon-lime carbonated beverage. Pour into 4 glasses and serve. Makes 4 servings.
● Reading suggestion:
Whinnie the Lovesick Dragon
   by Mercer Mayer

An Enchanted Forest

See pages 18 and 19

An enchanted forest is a good place to find hidden treasures like rocks or pebbles, and so is a sandbox. Sand also can be an exciting new art medium for your children to play with.

Make a cone out of heavy paper with a tiny hole at the point. Cover the small hole in the cone with your finger, then fill the cone with sand.

Now it's time for the kids. Show them how to move the cone around to make designs on a piece of dark paper. Then show them how to refill the cone with sand.

Glow Stones

See pages 20 and 21

The salt in the paint gives a crystalline look to the stones after the paint dries.

Salt Paint

> 2 tablespoons liquid starch
> 2 tablespoons water
> 1 tablespoon tempera paint *or* several drops liquid food coloring
> ½ cup salt

Stir together starch, water, and paint. Stir in salt. Stir the paint frequently during use.

Cozy Cottage

See pages 22 and 23

You can build one Cozy Cottage or a whole village. When you're done with that, try a Sweet Candy Palace. This model is made by sticking cinnamon graham crackers onto a milk carton frame coated with frosting.

For the base, cover a piece of cardboard with foil. Make the frame the height of the graham crackers by cutting two half-gallon milk cartons off near the bottom. Tape the milk cartons together side by side. Tape or staple the tops closed. Set the frame on the base.

Frost the frame with chilled canned frosting, then attach the crackers. For the roof, extend the crackers slightly over the edge of the frame for eaves. If desired, frost over the graham crackers on the roof and top with candies or cookies.

For the fence, use pretzel sticks held together with a small amount of frosting. If desired, pipe frosting onto the graham crackers for windows and doors and/or use colorful candies or cookies.
● Reading suggestions:
Rumpelstiltskin
   by Paul O. Zelinsky
The Great Blueness and Other Predicaments
   by Arnold Lobel

Fanciful Fortune-Tellers

See pages 24 and 25

Watching and listening to your children make believe is one of the highlights of parenthood. Encourage your children to pretend, and take part in their pretend games. By doing so, you are helping them to think, to see things as they want them to be, and to put themselves in someone else's position. All of this helps them learn to cope with and solve problems.

Shiny Crystal Ball

See pages 26 and 27

You can help your children get excited about the idea of fortune-telling by participating in the activity with them. Help them get into a mysterious mood and prompt them with ideas for fortunes. They're sure to have a great time after they see what it's all about.

Magic Ring and Necklace

See pages 28 and 29

Jazz up your jewelry collection with a brightly colored bracelet. Use the same candies and cereal you use for the Necklace *except* cut the shoestring licorice into 15-inch pieces.

Magic Tricks

Children are always begging to perform their newest magic trick for anyone who will watch. Here are a couple of simple tricks you can teach them to enhance their show.

The Magic Balloon: Blow up a balloon, then put 2 pieces of tape on the balloon to make an X. Carefully stick a pin through the middle of the X. The balloon won't pop because the tape holds it together.

(Remember to keep tape hidden from the audience.)

A Magic Hat: Ask a volunteer from the audience to balance a hat on a single piece of paper. After the volunteer has tried and failed, fold the paper back and forth like an accordion. Stand the pleated sheet on one side. Balance the hat on top of the paper. (Try this trick ahead of time so you can find the hat that works the best.)

BETTER HOMES AND GARDENS® BOOKS
Editor: Gerald M. Knox
Art Director: Ernest Shelton
Managing Editor: David A. Kirchner
Department Head, Family Life: Sharyl Heiken

MAKE BELIEVE
Editors: Jennifer Darling and Sandra Granseth
Graphic Designer: Linda Ford Vermie
Editorial Project Manager: Angela K. Renkoski
Contributing Illustrator: Buck Jones
Contributing Photographers: M. Jensen (cover), Scott Little
Contributing Graphic Designer: Patty Konecny
Project Consultant: Lisa Ann Bielser

Have BETTER HOMES AND GARDENS® magazine delivered to your door.
For information write to:
ROBERT AUSTIN
P.O. BOX 4536
DES MOINES, IA 50336